PUT
YOUR
ASS
(where your HEART wants to be)

Also by Steven Pressfield

PUT YOUR ASS

(where your HEART wants to be)

STEVEN PRESSFIELD

SARSAPARILLA MEDIA
(sar-sa-pa-rill-a)

Sarsaparilla Media LLC
Los Angeles, CA

Copyright © 2022 Steven Pressfield

Cover design by Diana Wilburn
Original cover photo by Bob Jensen

First Sarsaparilla Media Paperback Edition May 2022

For permission to reproduce selections from this book, write to:
Permissions, Sarsaparilla Media LLC
PO Box 2488, Malibu CA 90265

Paperback ISBN: 9798986164304
eBook ISBN: 9798986164311
Audiobook ISBN: 9798986164328

Book design by Evan Schoninger

Library of Congress Control Number: 2022910704

Printed in the United States of America.

www.stevenpressfield.com

FOR
DIANA

A NOTE TO THE READER

Who is this book for? What sort of person is a book called *Put Your Ass Where Your Heart Wants to Be* for?

It's for writers and artists and actors and Instagram chefs and podcasters and filmmakers and choreographers and video game creators and every kind of entrepreneur—whether your game is startups or nonprofits or your new Thai fusion restaurant.

In other words, it's for everyone who is *on their own in business or the arts*. And for everyone who *wants* to be on their own, who *dreams* of being on their own.

We all know how hard it is to write a book, make a movie, or create a new business. Powerful forces line up against us—obstacles to entry, rivals, competitors, finances, funding, the difficulty of the craft itself.

But the most formidable antagonist of all resides inside each of our own skulls. I'm talking about that negative force I call Resistance with a capital R.

What is Resistance? It's our own tendency—yours and mine and everyone's—to yield to procrastination, self-doubt, fear, impatience, self-inflation, self-denigration, distraction, laziness, arrogance, complacency, and perfectionism. It's our inability to focus, our incapacity to press on through adversity. It's our terror of finishing and exposing our work to the judgment of the marketplace. It's fear of failure. It's fear of success. Fear of humiliation. Fear of destitution. It's our inability to defer gratification, to acquire and act with self-discipline, self-validation, and self-reinforcement.

Resistance is our tendency to self-sabotage, fail to start, and fail to finish. In its most extreme forms, Resistance expresses itself as vice and even crime—abuse of ourselves or others, cruelty, addiction to substances, diva-ism, compulsive self-dramatization, self-aggrandizement and self-diminishment.

How do we defeat this monster that lives inside all of us and never tires, never loses strength, never takes a day off, and is endlessly ruthless and protean and subtle and clever and diabolical in the ways it can set snares for us and bring our most noble and brilliant aspirations to nothing? How do we get past this force called Resistance and set ourselves on the path to achieve our dreams?

The title of this book, as we said, is *Put Your Ass Where Your Heart Wants to Be*.

That, in nine words, is my answer. It's the simplest and most direct way to get up in the morning and do our work… and to lie down at night feeling at peace with ourselves, knowing for this one day at least we have defeated our demons and moved twenty-four hours closer to living the True Self and Best Self we were born to be.

Put Your Ass Where Your Heart Wants to Be may sound glib and superficial at first, but believe me, its implications are profound and its applications universal. We'll start, in this book, with the purely physical interpretation—"ass," meaning *body*, our flesh-and-blood presence. But as the chapters unfold, we'll take the subject deeper and deeper, into the psychological, the emotional, the metaphorical, and even the spiritual dimensions of this principle.

Let's begin.

Book One

PUT YOUR ASS WHERE YOUR HEART WANTS TO BE

Chapter 1

PUT YOUR ASS
WHERE YOUR HEART
WANTS TO BE

L et's start with the most obvious interpretation of this axiom. (We'll go deeper in succeeding chapters.)

What do we mean by "ass"? In the first-level interpretation, the word means *body*. Our physical presence. When we say, "Put your ass where your heart wants to be," we mean station your physical body in the spot where your dream-work will and must happen.

Want to write? Sit down at the keyboard.

Wanna paint? Step up before the easel.

Dance? Get your butt into the rehearsal studio.

Dumb and obvious as it sounds, tremendous power lies in this simple *physical action*.

When I sit down to write in the morning, I literally have no expectations for myself or for the day's work. My only goal is to put in three or four hours with my fingers punching the keys. I don't judge myself on quality. I don't hold myself accountable for quantity. The only questions I ask are, *Did I show up? Did I try my best?*

If I've done that, then I've put my butt where my heart wants to be. I can't ask anything of myself more than that.

Chapter 2

FEAR

What keeps us from writing or dancing or painting? If the process is as straightforward as we just described it, what's the big hang-up? Why doesn't everyone do it?

In one four-letter word: FEAR.

Yes, we're terrified to begin our eight-hundred-page Elizabethan family saga. When we sit over our morning coffee thinking about it, our palms sweat. Our heart palpitates in dread.

Get up! Go to your office! Don't stop to schmooze with your spouse or the dude in the next cubicle. Sit down! Open your file. Place your fingers on the keyboard.

Tremendous power lies in the simple, physical act of *stationing our body at the epicenter of our dream.*

There is magic in putting our ass where our heart wants to be.

Chapter 3

MOVE YOUR ASS TO WHERE YOUR HEART WANTS TO BE

Okay, we've accepted the idea of sitting down at the piano, of planting ourselves in the editing suite, of taking the "D" train to our dance studio.

Now let's take the principle a step further.

> Leave the town or city where you live and *move to the hub of the creative or entrepreneurial world where your dreams are most likely to come true.*

Let me repeat that.

> Pack up your total establishment—spouse, kids, dog, couch, treadmill—and move to the metropolis that's the epicenter of your career or creative dream.

Yes, I know we can all work remotely. Zoom will put our face before potential friends, mentors, and collaborators without us leaving the comfort of our home.

But it ain't the same as *being there.*

Someone may ask, "I want to work in country music. Do I have to move to Nashville?" Or "My dream is to act in movies. Do I have to pack up for LA?"

Yes and yes.

Chapter 4

THERE IS NOT HERE

Hemingway moved to Paris. Arnold Schwarzenegger left Austria for Gold's Gym in Venice, California. Bob Dylan moved to Greenwich Village. Joni Mitchell left Saskatoon for Laurel Canyon.

Why did they move? First: resources. In '68 there were no gyms like Gold's anywhere. If you wanted to be the best, like Arnold, you had to go where the resources were.

Want to make a feature film? Go where the cameras are.

Wanna be a ballet dancer? Yes, you can find good classes in Bozeman or Bogalusa. But the Joffrey and the ABT and the Met and the New York Ballet Company (and all the studios and schools that feed them) are in New York. The Royal Ballet is in London; the Ballets Russes is in Paris.

The Dalai Lama does not live in Terra Haute.

Chapter 5

MOVE, PART TWO

There's a second reason to pack up.

People.

You, the aspiring actress, may step off the bus in New York City friendless and alone. But six weeks later, after you've finished your first round of classes at the Actors Studio or the Neighborhood Playhouse, you'll have more sidekicks and BFFs than you know what to do with.

And these will not be friends like your buds back home, whose only contribution to your calling was to distract you and waste your time. These new friends share your dream. They'll make space for you in their fourth-floor walkup in Williamsburg. They'll share Ubers with you, and they'll help you get a job at the Shake Shack. They'll run lines with you before auditions.

In other words, these new friends are your true spiritual companions. They too have a dream—the same dream you have. They too have left home to pursue it. Like you, they are on the Yellow Brick Road.

They are your community. They will be your friends for life.

Chapter 6

FRIENDS AND MENTORS

Glenn Frey was the founding member of the Eagles along with Don Henley. He tells this story (I'm paraphrasing) in the documentary, *History of the Eagles.*

> I had moved to LA from Detroit. I was sharing a super-low-rent apartment in Silver Lake with J.D. Souther. We were struggling to establish ourselves as singers and songwriters. The apartment directly below us was Jackson Browne's. He was as broke and unknown as we were.

Frey describes how sound came up through the floor from Jackson Browne's place to his. All day he could hear Jackson Browne working on songs. Browne would play a song on the piano once, twice, thirty times. He'd stop to make himself a cup of tea (Glenn could hear the whistling teapot), and then he'd go back to the piano and work on the song for another thirty passes, tweaking it and revising it little by little.

> I realized, This is how you write a song! Not in one crazed pass, not scribbling notes and losing them in your jacket pockets or your glove compartment... but sitting down like a pro and working with the material, changing and improving the song over and over, until you had it exactly the way you wanted it.

I love this story because it illustrates how we all really learn. Friends. Role models. People we watch and copy.

But the key takeaway is that if Glenn Frey had not moved his ass from Detroit to Los Angeles, he would never have had the chance to cross paths with Jackson Browne—not to mention J.D. Souther and Don Henley and Linda Ronstadt and David Geffen and every one of the dozens of people whose friendship and wisdom helped take him to where his heart wanted to be.

Chapter 7

GURUS AND MASTERS

We've been speaking of "put your ass" in the sense of "move to a specific scene or metropolis." But there are other, more occult, applications of this principle.

Certain arts and skills may be learned only from a few masters—maybe as few as three or four in the whole world—whose academies or dojos may be located in the most remote places on Earth. To study Theravada Buddhism, you may have to travel to Katmandu. To study Zen via the art of archery, the young German philosopher Eugen Herrigel had to seek out master Awa Kenzo in Japan.

Big-wave surfing? There's Laird Hamilton and very few others. Show jumping or dressage? You may need to pack up for Germany to work with Klaus Balkenhol or Ernst Hoyos.

Even "The Bride," Beatrix Kiddo (Uma Thurman) in *Kill Bill, Volume Two* could learn the Five Point Palm Exploding Heart Technique only from the legendary master Pai Mei (Gordon Liu) at his remote Shaolin monastery.

The point, again, is there is no substitute for being there, at the heart of the action. And to get there, you have to leave "here."

Chapter 8

MOVE, PART THREE

Pick a few names at random from the acting pantheon (of course it's the same for writers, dancers, or videogame creators): James Dean, say, or Marlon Brando or Marilyn Monroe.

Most of them knew each other when they were twenty. They waited tables together. They borrowed money from each other. They stole each other's boyfriends and girlfriends. They studied at the Actors Studio.

Magic happens when we put our ass in the same space with other dreamers who have already put their asses there. These are our peers, our lovers, our fellow aspirants. What was it like to rehearse a scene from *Sweet Bird of Youth* with Paul Newman when he was twenty-one?

Hemingway in Paris gets to talk prose technique with Gertrude Stein and hang at the Closerie des Lilas with Lady Duff Twysden. Henry Miller in Montmartre can talk all night with Anais Nin and Blaise Cendrars. John Lennon in London can trade notes with Mick Jagger or turn down Eric Clapton for the gig that will go to George Harrison. None of that synergy would've happened if they'd all stayed home in Bushwick or Oak Park.

It's not enough for your heart to be in the right place. Your ass has to be there too.

Chapter 9
"HOW SOON CAN YOU BE HERE?"

There's no substitute for your physical presence at Ground Zero of your dream. I'm sorry, but you can't phone it in from the boonies unless you're already established, unless you have paid your dues and had your ticket punched.

When I decided to try and write for the movies, I packed up my Chevy van with my Smith-Corona and drove from New York to Los Angeles. It was the best move I ever made.

Why? Because when the phone rings at two in the morning and a frantic production assistant croaks in your ear, "Can you be at Paramount tomorrow at seven to help us fix act 2?", you can answer calmly, "I'll be there at 6:45."

But there's an even more critical reason to move your physical body to where your heart wants to be.

When you move your material ass to the geographic site of your dream, your peers and potential mentors think at once, *This person is serious. She has committed. She has burned the boats. She is one of us.*

Remember, the potential colleagues and decision-makers who can open doors for you... they've all already moved to Austin or Nashville or wherever the action in their/your field is hottest. They've moved to these places because *they're* serious. Because *they're* committed.

Yes, technically, you can audition via Zoom or send in your demo from fifteen hundred miles away, but you and your submission will not be considered as serious. You will be perceived as half-in/half-out, as a part-timer and a dilettante.

Chapter 10
HOW DOES SUCCESS (REALLY) HAPPEN?

My friend Ram Bergman is a big-time producer at the near-*Star Wars* level. When I first met him, twenty years ago, he was fetching coffee on movie sets for six bucks an hour.

How does success *really* happen?

Your friends help you. Friends you made when you and they were broke and starving. Your friends rise in their careers… and they bring you along.

Here's director Ernie Pintoff, advising me as a young screenwriter to plunge into the pool with no mental reservations.

> "Keep working," Ernie said. "Don't turn anything down. Porn flicks, slasher movies, free stuff for friends. Don't get precious. You're young. You're learning. Keep working."
>
> Ernie cited three reasons:
>
> "One, working means you're getting paid. Every buck means you're a working pro. You're toiling in your chosen field.
>
> "Two, when you work, you learn. Everybody has something to teach you. A grip will show you something about lighting, an editor will drop some pearl about what to keep and what to cut. Even actors know something.
>
> "Three, you're making friends. Some kid who's schlepping coffee today may be a producer tomor-

row. An actress you do some free work for today may get you hired for a rewrite six months from now."

This is how any career *really* works—dance, theater, photography, financial planning. Even the military works like this.

But before this network of friends and mentors can help you up the ladder, you have to be there. In person. In the flesh, where you can make these friends and find these mentors.

Chapter 11

NINE SCREENPLAYS

I had been in Los Angeles for about five years. I had written nine screenplays (each taking about six months) and sold none. I had a terrific agent and a great friend, Mike Werner.

Mike believed in me, but he was getting tired of taking my screenplays out to the town and having them sent back rejected. One day he took me out for coffee. "What would you think," Mike said, "about me teaming you up with an older, established writer? You'd be the junior member of the team… you'd have to work your ass off. But you'd be working. You'd get jobs. You'd be bringing home checks."

Mike teamed me with Ron Shusett, who had written the original *Alien* with his partner Dan O'Bannon, as well as *Total Recall,* that was making its way toward production at that time. Ron was a brand. He had had hits. He got us into meetings. Scripts we wrote on spec were taken seriously because his name was on the title page. For the first time in my life, I could actually pay the rent.

But the best part was what I learned working with Ron. I would throw ten ideas at him. He would discard nine and pick one… and he'd be right. He taught me how to evaluate material—what to keep and what to cut. He introduced me to the concept of acquiring and adapting. He opened my eyes to genres of film and literature—sci-fi, film noir, speculative fiction—that I had never even known about, let alone fallen in love with.

In Ron's company, I met other filmmakers—directors, editors, writers, financiers, studio people—from whom I learned even more and some of whom became real friends and allies that I still have today.

When I finally went out on my own, I felt like I'd acquired a PhD in film, just from the exposure working with Ron gave me.

Would I have met Ron if I'd stayed in New York? Would I have met Mike? Would I have met anybody?

Chapter 12

WHAT ABOUT OXFORD, MISSISSIPPI?

Oxford is where Faulkner lived. All his life. Stephen King resides in Maine and Sarasota, Florida. Anne Rice never left New Orleans or Rancho Mirage, California.

So let me modify the statement of the previous chapters. Let's carve out a special exemption for writers and other artists who can do their work in rustic cabins, poolside villas, and other abodes of seclusion and solitude.

We'll give their physical bodies a pass. But what about their metaphorical bodies?

These, I will make the case, *have* moved to the epicenter of their dreams.

Level One of Put Your Ass Where Your Heart Wants to Be is the physical dimension. Sit your body down in front of the keyboard. Or move your physical self to the city where your dream is most likely to find its home.

Level Two, however, is about the Inner Body, the metaphorical self. It means "move to the Paris/London/New York in your mind."

That, I venture to presume, has been done by Faulkner and Stephen King and Anne Rice. They have, in the metaphorical dimension, packed up bag and baggage and "moved" to that place in their hearts where their dream resides.

Depth of commitment.

Are you "there"? Or are you somewhere else?

Book Two

ASS = COMMITMENT

Chapter 13

ASS = COMMITMENT

We know what "ass" means in the physical sense. Let's examine it now as a metaphor.

"Ass" means *commitment*.

As in, "His ass is on the line." Or "If she screws this up, it'll be her ass."

When we say, "Put your ass where your heart wants to be" in this sense, we mean, "Commit emotionally, psychologically, spiritually to your dream."

In chapters 3 through 11, we urged the aspiring writer/filmmaker/chef/dancer to physically move to the city where her dreams have the best chance of coming true. But there's an even more compelling reason from the point of view of those established professionals who might hire or mentor or promote our newly arrived aspirant.

Our writer/filmmaker/chef/dancer has *demonstrated commitment*. She is *here*. She has left *there*.

She has shown that she is "crazy" in the best possible sense (as those established artists and entrepreneurs see themselves). She has demonstrated that she is driven by a dream. She has shown that she is willing to risk and sacrifice. She has proven she has guts.

Does it matter that, alone at a traffic light, our passionate dreamer finds herself breaking down in tears? Does it make a difference that she's terrified of the choice she has made, that she has to fight off nightly the overwhelming urge to pack up and go home?

All that matters is that she has taken action. She is *here*. She has left *there* behind.

This does not go unnoticed, by mortals or by the gods.

Chapter 14

WILL FRANK OZ HIRE US?

Film director Frank Oz (who's also the Muppet master behind Yoda and Miss Piggy) has a term for this all-in state of mind. He calls it "going the distance."

This is the test Frank applies at the start of any project—not just to himself but to anyone he will prospectively hire or collaborate with on a movie, a play, whatever.

Frank asks himself, "Will this person commit unconditionally to the work? Is this someone I can count on in act 3, when the wheels come off and the faint of heart flee for the exits? Is this someone who will have my back in crunch time?"

We're talking now about the third-level meaning of "Put your ass where your heart wants to be."

Commitment *over time.*

Commitment *in the face of adversity.*

When a movie director like Frank Oz takes on a project, he's projecting a two- or three-year commitment. He knows talent alone will not carry a collaborator that far. He wants troupers on his crew who will hang in, no matter what and no matter how long.

When you watch the credits on a picture by Joel and Ethan Coen or Quentin Tarantino or Martin Scorsese (or any top-flight enterpriser in any field), you'll often see the same names. Why? Because the director has *found his team.*

Through trial and error and time in grade, he or she has assembled a crew she can count on. Why is every Scorsese film edited by Thelma Schoonmaker? Why does Woody Allen work again and again with Jack Rollins and Santo Loquasto? These artists know their hand-picked homies will be standing tall at midnight on Doomsday.

Questions for ourselves:

"How much do we want it?"

"What sacrifices are we willing to make to see this project succeed?"

"Have we 'moved'—lock, stock, and barrel—to our inner Paris?"

SEB RESCUES MIA

There's a great sequence in the movie *La La Land,* written and directed by Damien Chazelle. The heroine Mia, played by Emma Stone, is shattered by the catastrophic failure of her one-woman show.

MIA
I'm going home.

SEB
I'll drive you.

MIA
No. Home.

Mia shelves her Hollywood dream and returns to her parents' house in Boulder City, Nevada. But Seb (Ryan Gosling) loves her and believes in her. When a possible break for Mia materializes, Seb drives to Boulder City, finds Mia's house (she had only told him it was "across from the library") and retrieves her by main force.

In a wonderful scene, he pulls up in front of her parents' house in his '73 Chevelle convertible, super early to get a head start on the drive back to LA. But Mia is not there. The house is dark. Seb has told Mia he will stop out front and if she's not waiting, he'll leave without her. He puts the Chevy into gear. In the audience, our hearts are sinking.

Suddenly Mia appears, hurrying, on foot, on the sidewalk. She carries a couple of take-out cups.

MIA
I just went to get us some coffees.

Sometimes it takes another person to believe in us. For Mia, it's Seb. In *tick, tick...BOOM!* that person for (the real life) composer Jonathan Larson was Stephen Sondheim.

The point is: That person seized our ass and dragged it back to where our heart wanted to be.

COMMITMENT = RISK

There's a term in mountaineering called "exposure." To be "exposed" means to be in a position where we can fall, possibly a long way, possibly to our death.

Exposure has an interesting twist. We can be ten meters from the summit of Everest, but if there's a nice, wide shelf two feet beneath us, we're not exposed. On the other hand, if we're only twenty feet above sea level but there's nothing but thin air beneath us, we're exposed.

Commitment = exposure. That's why people don't commit. They're not stupid. They don't want to risk falling off the mountain.

Chapter 17

THE KNOWN AND THE UNKNOWN

When we put our ass where our heart wants to be, we're taking a step that has terrified the human race since our days back in the cave.

Why is commitment so scary? Because when we commit, we're moving from the Known to the Unknown.

The definition of dream is that which exists only in our imagination. In other words, in the Unknown.

When we say, "Put your ass where your heart wants to be," we're proposing a mindset that is designed to outfox Fear of the Unknown. It says:

> Don't try to overcome your fear. Fear cannot be overcome. Instead simply *move your body into the physical space you fear…* and see what happens.

When we sprint barefoot across the ice floe and dive head-first into the frigid waters off Nordkapp, Norway, (yes, it's a real place) we have literally flung our goose-bumped, Speedo-clad flesh into the Unknown.

Inspiring, ain't it?

Chapter 18

COMMITMENT = POWER

The positive face of commitment is self-empowerment. The very act of putting our ass where our heart wants to be makes a profound impression, not just on those we wish to work with or be mentored by, but *on ourselves.*

When we shoulder our seabag and stride up the gangplank of the *Nina,* the *Pinta,* or the *Santa Maria,* something changes inside us. We might not feel it in the moment because our knees are knocking too violently. But somewhere deep in our DNA, a chemical transformation is taking place.

Are you familiar with the concept of the "hero's journey"?

In myth and legend, when the hero commits to an intention by taking bold action, he enacts a Cosmic Overthrow. He "crosses the threshold." Like Luke Skywalker heading with Obi-Wan Kenobi for Mos Eisley spaceport or Dorothy being swept away from Kansas by a cyclone, the hero moves from the Ordinary World to the Extraordinary World. She has gone from the Known to the Unknown.

Suddenly our hero sees herself differently. She can't help it. In *Wonder Woman,* the person Diana was when she followed her call and departed from her home on Themyscira is not the same person who had dwelt on this blessed isle since she was a child.

She is different now, and she knows it.

Chapter 19
THE UNIVERSE RESPONDS

I t is not an idle or airy-fairy proposition to declare that the universe responds to the hero or heroine who takes action and commits.

It responds *positively*.

It comes to the hero's aid.

Chapter 20
WHY DOES THE UNIVERSE RESPOND?

The Sphere of Potentiality—i.e., the dimension above the Material Plane—recognizes the alteration in our hero. She has changed. She is not the same person she was, even ten seconds earlier.

She has, by an act of will and love and daring, stepped out of the role of the passive and the self-paralyzed and into the role of the active protagonist, the hero. She has in fact *become* a hero, quaking knees notwithstanding.

The universe comes to the hero's aid.

Chapter 21

TOM GUINZBURG SAVES MY LIFE

When I first submitted my manuscript for *Gates of Fire*, it was eight hundred pages long. It weighed four pounds. It was as big as a Manhattan phone book. My agent, Sterling Lord, told me flat out, "Steve, I can't sell this. You have to cut three hundred pages."

Three hundred pages?

I was paralyzed. This was only my second book. I had no idea how to delete almost half of it and have it still work. I was shell-shocked; I fell into depression and despair.

Then I got a note in the mail—a hand-written note on personal stationery. The note was from Tom Guinzburg, who was then the president of Viking Press, one of New York's most prestigious publishing houses. Tom Guinzburg had been one of the founders of the *Paris Review,* along with George Plimpton and Peter Matthiessen. He was literary royalty, light-years above a novice like me.

It turned out that my agent Sterling had a weekly lunch with Tom and Larry Hughes of Wm. Morrow and other big guns of the New York publishing world. At Sterling's request, Tom had read the manuscript of *Gates of Fire*. His note to me said, among other kind things, "There is a first-rate novel in here. I am confident you will pull this off."

I can't tell you how much that meant to me. Tom Guinzburg barely knew me. There was no profit in it for him to reach out. He did it because he was a good guy with a generous heart.

That note changed my life. I taped it to the screen of my eight-bit Kaypro and took courage from it every day of the six months it took me to get three hundred pages out of that manuscript.

When you and I put our ass where our heart wants to be, the universe responds. We change. We see ourselves differently. But others, sometimes those we are not aware of (and whom we have no idea are aware of us), see us differently too. They may come to our aid in ways we could never have predicted and by some word or act of kindness change everything.

Chapter 22

THE UNIVERSE IS SELF-ORDERING

Imagine yourself back at the Big Bang. The universe is raw energy, blasting at the speed of light in all directions.

What happens? As time passes—maybe only nanoseconds—electrons coalesce around nuclei. Molten matter cools. Stars and planets form themselves into spheres. Celestial objects find paths and settle into orbits.

Order emerges.

On individual planets, gravity appears. Rivers form and run downhill. Seas arise. Atmospheres stabilize. Before you know it, we're witnessing adventurous fish crawling out onto dry land, hominids beating each other's brains out with rocks and clubs, and guys with pocket protectors doing IPOs for social networking startups.

What about your novel?

Books are self-organizing too. So are albums, entrepreneurial ventures, and statues of David. The process unfolds infallibly. Our symphony-in-the-works evolves into four movements, our screenplay orders itself into three acts.

If we just keep plugging away at it, the Law of Self-Ordering comes to our aid.

Work—day-in, day-out exertion and concentration—produces progress and order. That's a law of the universe.

Chapter 23

THE SCOTTISH HIMALAYAN EXPEDITION

But let's get back to help from others. I quoted part of the following passage in *The War of Art*. It's from *The Scottish Himalayan Expedition* by W. H. Murray (1951).

> ... but when I said that nothing had been done I erred in one important matter. We had definitely committed ourselves and were halfway out of our ruts. We had put down our passage money—booked a sailing to Bombay. This may sound too simple, but it is great in consequence. Until one is committed, there is hesitancy, the chance to draw back, always ineffectiveness.
>
> Concerning all acts of initiative (and creation), there is one elementary truth the ignorance of which kills countless ideas and splendid plans: that the moment one definitely commits oneself, then providence moves too. A whole stream of events issues from the decision, raising in one's favor all manner of unforeseen incidents, meetings and material assistance, which no man could have dreamt would have come his way. I have learned a deep respect for one of Goethe's couplets:
>
> Whatever you can do or dream you can, begin it.
> Boldness has genius, power and magic in it. Begin it now."

Book Three

PUT YOUR ASS...
OVER THE LONG HAUL

Chapter 24

COMMITMENT OVER TIME

So far in this book, we've been talking of "breaking in" to a field at the entry level. But "put your ass" is not a short-haul principle.

It applies lifelong.

Chapter 25
MY HERO, JAMES RHODES

Here's a passage from an article in the *Guardian UK* by James Rhodes, the concert pianist.

I didn't play the piano for ten years. A decade of slow death by greed working in the City, chasing something that never existed in the first place (security, self-worth [etc.]). And only when the pain of not doing it got greater than the imagined pain of doing it did I somehow find the balls to pursue what I really wanted and had been obsessed by since the age of seven—to be a concert pianist.

Admittedly I went a little extreme—no income for five years, six hours a day of intense practice, monthly four-day long lessons with a brilliant and psychopathic teacher in Verona, a hunger for something that was so necessary it cost me my marriage, nine months in a mental hospital, most of my dignity and about thirty-five pounds in weight. And the pot of gold at the end of the rainbow is not perhaps the Disney ending I'd envisaged as I lay in bed aged ten listening to Horowitz devouring Rachmaninov at Carnegie Hall.

My life [today] involves endless hours of repetitive and frustrating practising, lonely hotel rooms, dodgy pianos, aggressively bitchy reviews, isolation, confusing airline reward programmes, physiotherapy, stretches of nervous boredom (counting ceiling tiles backstage as the house slowly fills up) punctuated by short moments of extreme pressure (playing 120,000 notes from memory in the right order with the right fingers, the right sound, the right pedalling while chatting about the composers and pieces and knowing there are critics, recording devices, my mum, the ghosts of the past, all there watching), and perhaps most crushingly, the realisation that I will never, ever give the perfect recital. It can only ever, with luck, hard work and a hefty dose of self-forgiveness, be "good enough."

And yet. The indescribable reward of taking a bunch of ink on paper from the shelf at Chappell of Bond Street, tubing it home, setting the score, pencil, coffee and ashtray on the piano and emerging a few days, weeks or months later able to perform something that some mad, genius, lunatic of a composer three hundred years ago heard in his head while out of his mind with grief or love or syphilis. A piece of music that will always baffle the greatest minds in the world, that simply cannot be made sense of, that is still living and floating in the ether and will do so for yet more centuries to come. That is extraordinary. And I did that. I do it, to my continual astonishment, all the time.

I love this James Rhodes article because it captures so brilliantly and so economically—four short paragraphs—the passage that so many of us must go through before we find our calling and commit to living it out.

But it also shows duration of commitment.

James Rhodes is in this for life.

Chapter 26

HIGHWAY 61, ALL THE WAY

Remember Frank Oz's test for anyone he considers collaborating with? Is this person, Frank asks himself, capable of "going the distance"?

How would you say the artist below measures up?

Bob Dylan

The Freewheelin' Bob Dylan

The Times They Are a-Changin'

Another Side of Bob Dylan

Bringing It All Back Home

Highway 61 Revisited

Blonde on Blonde

John Wesley Harding

Nashville Skyline

Self Portrait

New Morning

Blood on the Tracks

Street-Legal

Slow Train Coming

Shot of Love

Infidels

Knocked Out Loaded

Oh Mercy

Good as I Been to You

World Gone Wrong

Time Out of Mind

Love and Theft

Modern Times

Together through Life

Tempest

Shadows in the Night

Fallen Angels

Rough and Rowdy Ways

When you and I put our ass where our heart wants to be, we do it for keeps. We're in it to the end of the line.

Chapter 27
A BODY OF WORK

I find it tremendously inspiring to view an artist's production in total, front to back, as a *body of work*.

Clouds

Both Sides Now

Ladies of the Canyon

Blue

For the Roses

Court and Spark

The Hissing of Summer Lawns

Hejira

Don Juan's Reckless Daughter

Mingus

Wild Things Run Fast

Dog Eat Dog

Chalk Mark in a Rain Storm

Night Ride Home

Turbulent Indigo

Taming the Tiger

Travelogue

Shine

When we consider Joni Mitchell's output in toto (and these albums are only a fraction of it), or Bob Dylan's, or that of any visionary or entrepreneur we can think of, it's impossible to imagine them doing anything else, isn't it?

Their themes are so strong, their obsessions so unquenchable, we can't help but think that if some force had compelled them to do anything other than produce these works, they would have died like a wild leopard penned in a cage.

Chapter 28
NO CHOICE

We can say of these artists, can't we (as we surely can of Philip Roth below), that they seem to have had no choice but to pursue these specific passions. They couldn't *not* produce these works.

Goodbye, Columbus

Letting Go

When She Was Good

Portnoy's Complaint

Our Gang

The Breast

The Great American Novel

My Life as a Man

The Professor of Desire

The Ghost Writer

Zuckerman Unbound

The Anatomy Lesson

The Prague Orgy

The Counterlife

Deception

Operation Shylock

Sabbath's Theater

American Pastoral

I Married a Communist

The Human Stain

The Dying Animal

The Plot Against America

Everyman

Exit Ghost

Indignation

The Humbling

Nemesis

Chapter 29

YOU HAVE A BODY OF WORK

You too have a body of work. It exists inside you, on the Plane of Potentiality.

Are you a writer? This body or work exists, like books on a bookshelf. Close your eyes. You can see them.

Are you a musician? These works exist like albums, like concerts, like performances. Listen with your inner ear. You can hear them.

These bodies of work exist as alternative futures. They are that which *can be…* and *should be…* and *want to be*.

But they are *not* that which is *guaranteed to be*.

A LIFETIME COMMITMENT

Can you put your ass where your heart wants to be for life?

A LIFETIME, ONE HOUR AT A TIME

Can we put our ass where our heart wants to be if we've got a family, a job, a mortgage?

Yes.

The Muse does not count hours. She counts commitment. It is possible to be one hundred percent committed ten percent of the time. The goddess understands.

James Patterson was creative director of J. Walter Thompson, the mega-ad agency of the fifties and sixties. His dream was to be a writer of fiction. He would come into the office every morning at six. He'd close his door and lock it. For two hours, he wrote fiction. When the advertising day started, he opened his door and became a regulation Mad Man.

As of 2022, James Patterson's books have sold three hundred million copies.

One hour a day is seven hours a week, thirty hours a month, 365 hours a year. Three hundred and sixty hours is nine forty-hour weeks.

Nine forty-hour weeks is a novel. It's two screenplays, maybe three.

In ten years, that's ten novels or twenty movie scripts.

You can be a full-time writer, one hour a day.

Chapter 32

IT'S NOT HABIT. IT'S YOUR LIFE.

I have a trainer at the gym. His name is T.R. Goodman. You can look him up.

One day I said something to him about habit as it pertains to working out. He shook his head.

"It's not habit. It's your life."

T.R. is right. At some point the practice of our vocation moves from being a challenge that we must will ourselves into accepting and enacting to becoming simply... our life.

Like a mother raising her children or a farmer tending his crops.

This is our calling.

This is who we are.

This is what we do.

Book Four

PUT YOUR ASS…
IN A SPACE

Chapter 33

COMMIT TO A SPACE

When I was eight, my family spent part of a summer visiting friends in New England. One of the grownups was a painter. He had a big sunny studio out behind the house.

I remember the artist's wife admonishing me and my brother Mike, "Don't ever go in there without Peter's permission."

Of course, Peter gave his permission all the time. He was happy to have kids around. Sometimes we even took naps in his studio.

One thing we were always careful of, though, was not to make noise. And not to distract Peter when he was working.

His studio was a sacred space.

Later, when I studied martial arts, the sensei insisted that his students stop and bow before they crossed the threshold of the dojo—to him as our teacher and to the space itself.

It too was sacred.

My own office today is just a converted bedroom. It's got nothing esoteric in it, except maybe my lucky toy cannon that fires inspiration into me or perhaps my lucky horseshoe from Keeneland in Lexington, Kentucky.

But it's a sacred space too.

I've made it sacred by the work I've done there and by the attitude of respect and devotion I bring with me when I enter. Kids can come in. Animals can hang out. But they have to be respectful too, as I and my brother were when we crossed the doorstep of Peter the painter's studio.

Chapter 34

COMMIT TO A TIME

The legend of Hunter S. Thompson has him banging out fiction on an Olivetti portable in the passenger seat of a '67 Corvette crossing the Mojave at 160 miles per hour while out of his mind on Owsley window-pane acid.

On the other hand, I have it on very good authority that when Mr. T had a deadline to meet, he was as disciplined as Krishnamurti and as on time/on target as Chuck Yeager.

The goddess doesn't just want to know where we are. She wants to know what time we start and at what hour we finish.

How can she come to our aid if she doesn't know where and when to find us?

Chapter 35

COMMIT TO A LEVEL OF CONCENTRATION

My friend and mentor David Leddick wrote this of his days as a young dancer in New York City…

> I studied ballet at the Metropolitan Opera when Margaret Craske was the star teacher. Miss Craske instructed us: "Leave your problems outside the classroom."
>
> In that hour and a half of intense concentration on every part of your body, the music, the coordinating with the other dancers, you really couldn't think about your troubles and it was great escaping them.
>
> We worked hard. We never had a sick day. You went on even if you had to lie down in the wings until you were needed. No one thought this was unusual.
>
> In later careers all this has stood me in good stead. I never had to work that hard in any of the various worlds I later entered.

When we put our ass where our heart wants to be, we simultaneously exclude everything that is *not* about our work and our heart.

Chapter 36

TELAMON INSPECTS THE TROOPS

The following is from my novel about Alexander the Great, *The Virtues of War*. The narrator in this scene is Alexander as a boy. "Telamon" is a sergeant in Alexander's father Philip of Macedonia's army.

> I remember looking on as a lad of eleven, when Telamon (serving then under my father) formed up his company prior to the first march-out against the Triballians. He ordered each trooper to unshoulder his pack and set it upright at his feet. Telamon then proceeded down the line, rifling each kit, discarding every item of excess. When he was done, the men had nothing left beside their weapons but a clay cup, an iron spit, and a *chlamys* cloak and blanket.
>
> There are further items, Telamon taught, which have no place in the soldier's kit. Hope is one. Thought for future or past. Fear. Remorse. Hesitation.

Telamon went Miss Craske one better. The men under his command were to leave behind not only their individual problems, but every thought, belief, or attitude that would not serve them in the field. He meant,

Leave your ego, leave your greed, leave your competitiveness with your comrades, leave your lust for glory and your fear and your self-doubt and your lack of belief in yourself. Leave everything but your will to victory.

Chapter 37

COMMIT TO A LEVEL OF ASPIRATION

What would it be like to train as a quarterback beside Tom Brady?

How hard would we have to work to practice alongside Steph Curry?

How would we feel submitting our manuscript to Maxwell Perkins, who edited Hemingway and Scott Fitzgerald?

When we say, "put your ass," we mean put it *at the highest possible level.*

Chapter 38
COMMIT WITHOUT A PLAN B

I'm sometimes asked, "How did you keep going all those years without any success?"

I couldn't have answered at the time, except to say that I had no choice. Any time I tried to take the intelligent course, i.e., get a real job, I became so depressed I couldn't stand it.

One time I had quit a job in advertising. My boss, who was a good guy, was giving me a ride, after my last day, to the Bronx garage where I kept my ancient Chevy van. I was driving to California the next day to write yet another novel that nobody would publish. As we drove up the FDR Drive along the East River we passed a homeless guy, humping his backpack, with a poncho over his shoulders in the rain.

"Yeah, Steve," my boss said. "That'll be you in a few months."

My boss wasn't trying to be mean. He was speaking the truth.

I didn't care. I had no choice. I couldn't go back to the office. I'd have had to hang myself.

I had to keep going.

Chapter 39

COMMIT EVEN WHEN IT'S BOGUS

I was in a production meeting at Warner Bros. for the second Steven Seagal movie, *Hard to Kill*. It was called *Seven Year Storm* then. The director was Bruce Malmuth.

The screenplay had a car chase in it. The film was low-budget and the sequence was scripted very tightly. Bruce however had come up with a new idea—a way to make the chase different and original, something no one would expect in a "B" movie. But he needed more money from the studio and an extra day of shooting. I remember Bruce rising from his seat and making an impassioned plea for just a few more bucks and a little extra time.

The Warners' executive listened attentively. Bruce sat back down. He was actually out of breath from delivering his fervent appeal. The exec thanked Bruce for his commitment and his creativity. He saluted him as a dedicated filmmaker and a true artist. Then he said:

> "Bruce, think of this movie as a sausage. It's just another link and you're grinding it out."

Everyone around the table, including Bruce, burst into laughter. But we all felt a chill too, at hearing the reality of the marketplace stated in such stark, unvarnished terms. I remember thinking at the time,

The executive is right. This movie is a sausage. And we are here to grind it out.

But my attitude toward the process, I thought, does not have to be cynical or condescending. In fact, I am grateful as hell to be here working on this sausage and to have a chance to grind it out.

And furthermore:

Nobody, including the studio and the studio exec, can stop me from giving my all to make it the best sausage possible.

In the end, I got fired off the picture. You won't find my name in the credits. But I still agree with what I thought then.

Every project doesn't have to be *Citizen Kane*. It's okay to work on "B" movies and "C" pictures or to write trade ads for Preparation H. As long as we do our absolute best and keep our eyes on the prize of producing, maybe five or ten years from now, our own best material, as truly as we can to our own lights.

Chapter 40
COMMIT TO SERVING HEAVEN

The first thing I do when I enter my office each morning is say a prayer to the Muse. I say it out loud in dead earnest.

The prayer I say (this is in *The War of Art*, page 119) is the invocation of the Muse from Homer's *Odyssey*, translation by T.E. Lawrence, the Oxford-educated classical scholar also known as "Lawrence of Arabia."

When we commit fully to our calling, we acknowledge the forces of inspiration that we hope to summon to our aid. For me, this prayer is part of that process.

The prayer was given to me by one of my first writing mentors, Paul Rink. He typed it out on his ancient manual Remington and gave it to me. I still have it. The paper is so worn and crinkled it looks like parchment.

But the prayer itself is indelible.

I can't compel the goddess to appear. I can't bribe her, or coerce her, or grovel before her, or make her any pledges or promises that will induce her to do what I wish.

I can only invoke her.

That's what Homer was doing when he began the *Odyssey* with these verses:

> O, Divine Poesy,
> Goddess, daughter of Zeus,
> sustain for me this song ...

He did the same in the *Iliad*, with:

> Sing, goddess,
> of the wrath of Achilles, Peleus' son ...

I'm doing my work the same way the crypt carvers of Petra did theirs, or the musicians in the court of Louis XIV, or Hemingway and Gertrude Stein in Paris in 1921.

I'm doing it the same way Homer did and by the same rules.

THIS IS THE DAY

H ere's my frame of mind as I sit down to work:

This is the day. There is no other day. This is the day.

In other words, I release every thought that smacks of, "Maybe we can do this some other time."

There is no other time.

Today is the Superbowl.

Today is the day I give birth.

Today is the day I die.

Chapter 42
THIS IS THE JOB

This is the job. There is no other job. This is the job.

Chapter 43

COMMIT TO NO DISTRACTIONS

It goes without saying, I have turned off all external sources of distraction.

No phone.

No e-mail.

No Instagram.

No Facebook.

I am on an ice floe in Antarctica. I'm circling alone at seventy thousand feet. I'm on the moon.

Barring a nuclear attack or a family emergency, I will not turn my attention to anything that's not happening inside my own demented brain.

Chapter 44
TIME FLIES

When we have put our ass—our commitment—where our heart wants to be, time itself changes. From *The War of Art:*

It is a commonplace among artists and children at play that they're not aware of time or solitude while they're chasing their vision. The hours fly. The sculptress and the tree-climbing type both look up blinking when Mom calls, "Suppertime!"

Chapter 45
WHEN THE WHISTLE BLOWS

I stop working when I start making mistakes. Typos and misspellings tell me I'm tired. I have reached the point of diminishing returns.

Steinbeck said he always wanted to leave something in the well for tomorrow. Hemingway believed you should stop when you knew what was going to happen next in the story.

You and I, as writers and artists, are playing always for tomorrow. Our game is the long game.

When you're tired, stop.

Chapter 46
THE OFFICE IS CLOSED

When I finish the day's work, I turn my mind off.

The office is closed.

The work has been handed off to the Unconscious, to the Muse. I respect her. I give her her time.

If I see family or friends, I *never* talk about what I'm working on. I politely deflect any queries. But beyond not talking with others, I refuse to talk to myself. I don't obsess. I don't worry. I don't second-guess.

I let it rest.

The office is closed.

Chapter 47

GETTING READY FOR TOMORROW

The last thing I do before closing my eyes is to mentally prepare for the fight tomorrow.

Indeed, I have put my ass where my heart wants to be *today*.

That's not enough.

I am playing the long game. I am inculcating habit. I am deepening my practice and my commitment, day by day, day after day.

I'm training myself and reinforcing myself every day.

THE GODDESS VISITS AT NIGHT

I said the office is closed. That's not completely accurate. I set my phone or my mini-recorder on my bedside table. You never know who might drop in overnight.

Book Five

FORTUNE FAVORS THE BOLD

Chapter 49
THE MUSE KNOWS

The goddess is like Santa Claus. She knows when we've been naughty or nice.

I'm not being facetious.

Somehow, by some mechanism unknown and unknowable to mortals, the Higher Dimensions see and know what's going on down here on the Material Plane.

When you and I put our ass you-know-where, the Muse notices. And she responds.

Chapter 50
WISDOM OF THE STOICS

I'm a big fan of Ryan Holiday and his blog/books/podcasts about the ancient Stoics and the principles of Stoicism. But I do have one bone to pick with him and with them.

The primary principle of Stoicism, as I understand it, is that Fortune is unknowable, unpredictable, and for sure uncontrollable. The proper province of a Stoic, therefore, is to strengthen herself mentally and emotionally so the inevitable glories and catastrophes of life do not cause her to unravel or to act in a manner unworthy of her highest self.

Who can argue with that? But here is where, as Sir John Gielgud declared to Ben Cross in *Chariots of Fire*, "our paths diverge."

I think you *can* influence Fortune, if by Fortune we mean the unknowable will and actions of heaven. I believe our actions here on the mortal plane not only do not go unnoticed by the Plane of Potentiality, but that there is a direct (if still unfathomable) connection.

In fact, our mantra—Put your ass where your heart wants to be—implies exactly that.

Chapter 51

THE ILIAD

Did you read the *Iliad* in college? One aspect of that greatest of all epics that often goes unremarked (understandably enough, amid the human drama and carnage) is the presence of the gods. They're everywhere.

Athena, wishing to change Odysseus' mind, appears to him in a dream.

Aphrodite, to save her favorite, the Trojan prince Paris, deflects an arrow that would have slain him... and then sends an obscuring mist that allows him to escape safely from the battlefield.

Achilles' immortal mother, the nymph Thetis, "clasps the knees of Zeus" in supplication for her son.

Was Homer being whimsical or airy-fairy? Or did he know something you and I don't?

Chapter 52
THE BHAGAVAD GITA

I n this timeless scripture of India, the great warrior Arjuna re-
ceives spiritual counsel from his charioteer, Krishna, i.e., God
in human form.

> He who watcheth me everywhere,
> I watch him always.
> He never loses sight or me
> Nor I lose sight of him.

This statement by Krishna is a declaration of the indissever-
abilty of the mortal plane and the Immortal.

> Those who worship lesser teachers go unto them.
> My devotees, Arjuna, come unto me.

The *Bhagavad-Gita,* like the *Iliad,* posits a reality in which
gods inhabit the same material dimension as mortals. Not only do
these deities interact with their human compatriots, but they ac-
tively aid and support them. The interesting part, to me at least,
is that when we read and imagine this reality, it doesn't seem out-
landish at all. We accept it as, if not literally within our own experience, then certainly imaginable. We believe it.

Why?

My answer is because this depiction of reality rings a bell
with us. On some level, conscious or unconscious, it sounds true.

I'm not getting religio-nutty on you, I promise. I'm merely suggesting that the idea that the Higher and Lower Dimensions interact and communicate has been stated and believed by greater minds than yours and mine.

Could it be possible that you and I can influence the Muse?

Chapter 53

FORTUNE FAVORS THE BOLD

The seminal action of every pitched battle fought by Alexander the Great was his headlong charge, mounted on his great warhorse Bucephalus, into the teeth of the enemy. Alexander wore distinctive armor and a double-plumed helmet so that his rush, at the head of his sixteen-hundred-strong Companion Cavalry, would be missed by no one on the field.

Why did Alexander risk his life like this? First and most certainly, to inspire his men. Alexander believed that the sight of their king charging fearlessly at the foe would compel the warriors of his own phalanx and auxiliary cavalry to emulation, that they would follow their champion's example and attack with equal fire and passion.

But Alexander believed something greater. His conviction was that heaven, witnessing his act of valor and fearlessness, would be compelled to act as well. The heart of Zeus (or whatever we might call chance, luck, fortune) could not look on unmoved. The Higher Dimension would intervene, somehow, some way, in Alexander's favor.

Fortune, Alexander believed, favors the bold.

Chapter 54

YOUR SYMPHONY

What does all this have to do with you and me on planet Earth?

It means that putting our ass where our heart wants to be is the equivalent of Alexander charging into the breach at the Granicus River or at Issus or Gaugamela.

We too are risking all. We too hold nothing back. We too have hurled ourselves headlong into the unknown.

Heaven sees this. The Muse knows. You, the standup comic, suddenly find yourself entering areas of politics or sex you never thought you could. You, the screenwriter, discover your two-person love story expanding into a multi-generational epic. You, the dancer, the third baseman, the wide receiver, find you can play through that plantar fasciitis or that tweaked hamstring.

I believe heaven notices. The universe is not indifferent.

Book Six

PUT YOUR ASS...
AND KEEP IT THERE

Chapter 55

REINFORCEMENT AND SELF-REINFORCEMENT

L et me start this chapter with what may seem like an over-statement:

> For writers and artists, the ability to self-reinforce is more important than talent.

What exactly *is* reinforcement?

It's when your coach or mentor tugs you aside and tells you how well you are doing, how proud of you they are, and how certain they are that ultimate success will be yours if you just stay who you are and keep doing what you're doing.

That's reinforcement.

Can you tell *yourself* that? Without a coach? Without a mentor? Can you be your own coach and mentor?

That's self-reinforcement.

When we say, "Put your ass where your heart wants to be," we also mean *keep it there.*

Self-reinforcement keeps us there. It keeps us committed over the long haul.

I'll say it again:

> For writers and artists, the ability to self-reinforce is more important than talent.

Now: What are some of the principles of self-reinforcement?

Chapter 56

WATASHI DON'T CARE HOW YOU "FEEL"

I had a sergeant in the Marine Corps whose influence on me remains powerful to this day. This was at Camp Lejeune in what is called now the School of Infantry but in those days was ITR, Infantry Training Regiment.

This particular sergeant had survived two tours in Vietnam, so he possessed abundant cred with us young Marines he was training. He had spent time on Okinawa as well and had picked up a smattering of Japanese. Primary among his vocabulary was the word *Watashi*. I've been informed since that Watashi simply means "I." But the way our Watashi employed it, it meant "boss" or "head honcho."

Our sergeant always referred to himself in the third person. He was "Watashi." He insisted that we address him that way. "Yes, Watashi. Anything you say, Watashi." To this day I have no idea what Watashi's real name was.

Watashi's implement of enforcement was a pool cue. He carried one with him at all times. He would swat you with it broadside, across your back or the backs of your thighs. Or he'd jam you in the belly with the butt end. One time I saw him sling his pool cue sidearm, end-around-end, from the top of an elevated gunnery tower. Fortunately, the young Marine he hit was wearing his helmet.

But another lesson Watashi taught has stuck with me to this day. Watashi always pronounced the word "feel" as if it had quotation marks around it. In other words, he scorned the word absolutely.

In Watashi's lexicon, *feel* and *feelings* had no meaning in war. They had no meaning in competition. They had no meaning in life.

> "Watashi don't give a shit how you 'feel.' The Marine Corps don't give a shit how you 'feel.' Did the Marine Corps issue you 'feelings,' dirtball? Then you ain't got none."

All that mattered to Watashi was that you *do your job*—on time and to the best of your ability—whether you "felt" like it or not.

How do I apply Watashi's wisdom today? If I don't "feel" like getting out of bed in the morning, I hear and see a Little Watashi in my mind's eye. I dismiss that "feeling" and get up.

I dismiss positive feelings too, at least as they affect work. If I'm self-satisfied or in soaring good spirits and want to celebrate or take the day off, I place those feelings as well in quotation marks. I have internalized Watashi and even, in my imagination, his pool cue.

> Watashi don't give a shit how you "feel." Did the Marine Corps issue you "feelings"? Then you ain't got none. Shut up and get to work!

That's self-reinforcement.

Chapter 57

SELF-REINFORCEMENT = REALITY CHECK

Sometimes when circumstances seem overwhelming, when we find ourselves in a world of confusion and despair, self-reinforcement can take the form of a reality check.

We sit still. We take a breath. "Probably," we tell ourselves, "that asteroid will not strike the Earth next week, destroying all life as we know it. Nor does that letter from the IRS mean we will soon be imprisoned for tax evasion. Take a walk around the block, Steve. Things are not as bad as you're imagining them."

That, too, is self-reinforcement.

Chapter 58

A DIFFERENT DEFINITION OF REALITY

O n the other hand, "reality" can sometimes be a symptom of Resistance.

Often, "reality" means nothing more than *conventional* reality. And conventional reality is almost always wrong. Ask Dick Rowe of Decca Records, who turned down the Beatles.

Henry Miller worked as a supervisor for the phone company in Brooklyn. In *Tropic of Capricorn,* he called it the Cosmodemonic Telegraph Company of North America. Charles Bukowski worked for years for the Post Office. Can you imagine how "reality" was defined for them by their bosses and by the expectations of others?

What was reality? It was that these guys were great writers struggling to find their voices and become the gifts-to-the-world they truly were.

Sometimes self-reinforcement means kicking "reality" out the door and replacing it with Reality.

> "Hey, Tom! This is yourself speaking. Yes, you were drafted #199 in the sixth round of the 2000 NFL draft. Yes, six other quarterbacks were taken before you. Screw that 'reality'! We will show every general manager who didn't draft you that they were blind. Believe me when I tell you, Tom, that one day you will become a household name—the GOAT, the Greatest of All Time, with *seven* Super Bowl rings,

five Super Bowl MVP trophies, and three league MVP awards. Now *that's* Reality."

That's self-reinforcement.

Chapter 59

A SUPERPOWER

Self-reinforcement is a superpower.

It may seem silly when it's enacted in the moment—some crazy waitress/actress talking to herself in her Honda at a stop light.

But in fact that young lady has put her ass where her heart wants to be… and she has found the self-talk and self-validation to *keep it there*.

Chapter 60

REALITY WITH A CAPITAL R

Surely on the night before a battle, Alexander the Great in his private heart must have thought something like this:

> Am I crazy? Do I really intend, tomorrow, to charge into the teeth of the enemy, mounted on my warhorse Bucephalus, who is recognizable on sight by every man of the foe while I myself am dressed in distinctive armor, wearing a double-plumed helmet so that every warrior on the opposing side knows it's me? Every enemy arrow is going to be aimed at me, every javelin, every lance, every sling bullet. The greatest champions of the foe will all rush straight at me, seeking to win glory by being the one to slay me. Am I out of my mind to put myself in such a position?

Surely Alexander's comrades seconded this. "Don't risk yourself, Sire! We need you! What will the army do if you are killed?"

That was reality. Objective assessment. Who could argue with it? Yet...

Yet there existed simultaneously—and Alexander, beyond all others, was aware of it—a second reality.

In this second Reality, Alexander's seemingly reckless charge made absolute sense. Its audacity would strike terror into the hearts of the enemy. Its valor would inspire his own men and incite them to charge alongside him. And, in Alexander's mind, the boldness of the stroke would invoke heaven's aid and intercession.

What proof do we have that Alexander's Reality possessed substance? He survived and prevailed in four of the greatest battles in history—the Granicus River, Issus, Gaugamela, and the Battle of the Hydaspes River in India—as well as literally scores of others. He had conquered the Persian Empire, the greatest in history up to that time, by the time he was twenty-five. By thirty, Alexander had reached the limits of the known world. He was never defeated.

"IN TRUTH I AM A WARRIOR-PRIEST…"

Can you stand one more chapter about Alexander?

The following comes from *The Virtues of War*. The speaker is Alexander.

> I felt at home in Egypt. I could happily have been a priest. In truth I am a warrior-priest, who marches where Heaven directs him, in the service of Necessity and Fate. Nor is such a notion vain or self-infatuated. Consider: Persia's time has passed. In the Invisible World, Darius' empire has already fallen. Who am I, except the agent of that end, which already exists in the Other World and at whose birth I assist in this one?

What fascinates me about the character of Alexander the Great is that he seemed to see the future with such clarity and such intensity as to make it virtually impossible that it would not come true—and that he would be the one to make it so.

That's you and me at the inception of any creative project.

The book/screenplay/nonprofit/start-up already exists in the Other World.

Your job and mine is to bring it forth in this one.

Chapter 62

KEATS' "NEGATIVE CAPABILITY"

The great Romantic poet John Keats (1795-1821) had a different notion of self-reinforcement. The following is from a letter to his brother George (who was quite a character in his own right) in 1817:

> I had not a dispute but a disquisition with Dilke, upon various subjects; several things dove-tailed in my mind, and at once it struck me what quality went to form a Man of Achievement, especially in Literature, and which Shakespeare possessed so enormously—I mean Negative Capability, that is, when a man is capable of being in uncertainties, mysteries, doubts, without any irritable reaching after fact and reason ...

Put in slightly less deathless prose, the poet's thought might go like this:

> "Hey, John! This is John speaking. Those doubts you're experiencing about *Endymion?* I know you think you're never going to finish such an epic. I know you're afraid the work will be savaged in the *Times.* They'll say you're not fit to hold Percy Shelley's quill pen or Lord Byron's sheet of parchment. BS, baby! I'm here to tell you, your poem is great!

Scholars will be poring over its stanzas for centuries. Lovers will be cadging verses and dispatching them to their beloveds. Buck up, buddy! The tunnel may seem dark right now, but keep plugging. Don't lose faith. You will emerge from it—I promise—to the sunlit uplands of poetic glory and renown!"

Chapter 63
SELF-REINFORCEMENT AND DREAMS

I'm starting a new book now and Resistance is beating the hell out of me.

The book is nonfiction. Autobiographical. Here's the form Resistance is taking. It's telling me (the voice in my head, that is),

> "What are you, crazy, Steve? Do you imagine any-body is gonna be interested in these lame-ass stories from your life? They are so *ordinary! You* are so or-dinary. Readers are going to laugh you off the page. Whatever credibility you've built up over the years will go straight into the toilet. Stop right now before you totally humiliate yourself!"

Worse, I'm utterly confused by the way the book is coming to me. No chapter seems to follow another. It's all a jumble. I'm hopelessly lost.

In the midst of this, I had the following dream (verbatim from my notes to myself):

> Somehow I got into my possession a diary/journal of Hemingway's that he had used during the writing of a novel. Not a specific diary from real-life, just one in the dream. The journal was in the form of hand-drawn maps with no text. Each map (there was a big pile of them) represented one day's writing.

The idea was that Hemingway was driving across country east to west and each day's travel represented one day's writing. Except the maps were ridiculously vague—no place names, no road numerals, no river names, nothing. I studied the pages one at a time trying to figure out what state/city/road they represented. I assumed Hem was starting from Boston or Maine (not sure why I assumed this, it just made sense in the dream) so I'd look at a map page and ask myself, "Is this Massachusetts? Is this Connecticut?" But I couldn't tell. Farther west, I asked myself, "Is this body of water the Hudson? Is this Lake Champlain?" It was impossible to tell. The maps themselves seemed a little off, like no body of water was reliably the Hudson.

My analysis/conclusion:

The dream was trying to tell me to keep the faith regarding the crazy way this book is unspooling. It, the dream, is invoking Keats' idea of Negative Capability. If I think of writing this book as a trip east to west across the United States, each day I'm lost. My maps don't tell me where I am. Middle of book? End? But don't worry, says the dream. Hemingway did it this way, and it worked for him.

Chapter 64

THE UNCONSCIOUS IS THE ORGAN
OF SELF-REINFORCEMENT

You and I have a mentor in our heads.

This mentor is our Self, in the Jungian sense. It is the Greater Psyche—the Unconscious—from which come dreams, intuitions, and inspiration.

The dream above reinforced me and gave me courage as powerfully as if Gandalf and Merlin and Obi-Wan Kenobi had appeared in my driveway and delivered the same positive message.

The Unconscious is the organ of self-reinforcement.

Book Seven

PUT YOUR ASS…
OUT THERE IN PUBLIC

Chapter 65
ENTERING THE SPACE

M y friend Jack Carr is a former Navy SEAL sniper who
made the transition, seemingly seamlessly, to bestselling
thriller writer (*The Terminal List, Savage Son, In the Blood.*)
When I asked Jack how he did it, he said,

> I decided if I was going to enter the space, I was go-
> ing to enter it in full force.

What we're talking about here is *breadth of commitment.*

It's not just put your ass. It's put your *whole* ass. And put it
across the *full spectrum.*

My own weakness, forever, has been promoting myself and my
books. I've been great at putting my ass into the writing part, but
I've dropped the ball big-time in marketing and self-promotion.

Not so with Jack. He has entered the space with all guns blazing.

Jack doesn't just write the books. He has a podcast, he has a
blog, and he has a store. You can buy a mug, a hat, a crossed-tom-
ahawks wallet, a T-shirt. When a new novel appears, Jack is on
the road, virtually if not physically. He does interviews, he runs
contests, he gives away samples of the new book, and he creates
VIP packs complete with souvenirs and cool little premiums.

Jack appears regularly on cable news. He has made himself
a go-to authority on issues involving the military, especially the
mindset of the warrior and the transition of veterans to civilian
life. Jack is present constantly on social media—and always "on-
brand." Even his beard is on-brand. You will see him on Insta-

gram and Facebook at outdoor or shooting events, in extreme weather and endurance conditions. He has a book club. He supports independent bookstores and booksellers.

Jack has sponsors. The hero of his thrillers is James Reece, who shares much of Jack's Navy SEAL background and his expertise with weapons and tactics. Jack's co-branders include knife-makers and crafters of edged weapons. Sig Sauer provides prizes for contests that Jack runs to promote his books, as do Black Rifle Coffee, Yeti, Winkler Knives and many others.

You may say this is overkill or crass commercialism. But Hemingway did it, in the manner of his era, via *LIFE* magazine and a thousand gossip-column tales of big-game hunting in Africa, sport-fishing in the Florida Keys, and war correspondent work all over. Norman Mailer was everywhere in his heyday, as was Philip Roth and Tom Wolfe and scores of others.

These days, of course, a branding presence is even more indispensable to an artist or entrepreneur. Can we do it? Are we intimidated? Are we too shy or introverted? Too proud?

You and I can't put *half* our ass where our heart wants to be. We have to be in all the way.

Chapter 66

ARE YOU AFRAID TO SELL YOURSELF?

I am.

When my novel *A Man at Arms* came out in 2020, I bit the bullet and flung myself into "the space," as my friend Jack Carr would say. One wall in my office was covered with 3X5 index cards, each one representing a podcast I would appear on.

Let me tell you: I was waaaay out of my comfort zone.

These days, alas, there is no choice. For a writer, it's about fidelity to the book and, especially, to the characters. You have to be their champion. They can't do it themselves. You have to be the one to help them have their day in the sun.

There is no worse feeling for a writer or any artist than to see her book, her film, her music go out there and die. Or worse, be launched into the world and nobody even knows it exists. I've experienced this more than once and it's heartbreaking.

Chapter 67

SEA OF DARKNESS

The following is from *The War of Art:*

> I had a dear friend who had labored for years on an
> excellent and deeply personal novel. It was done. He
> had it in its mailing box. But he couldn't make him-
> self send it off. Fear of rejection unmanned him.

The story has an even sadder ending. My friend died. No one
except me and a few close companions and family even know the
book existed.

Chapter 68

PUT YOUR ASS ALL THE WAY TO THE FINISH LINE

From Ryan Holiday's *Perennial Seller:*

> You can cut back on a lot of things as a leader, but
> the last thing you can ever skimp on is marketing.
> Your product needs a champion... That must be you.
> Marketing is your job. It can't be passed on to some-
> one else. Even if you're famous, even if you have a
> million Twitter followers, even if you have a billion
> dollars to spend... it's still on you and it still won't
> be easy.

Putting your ass where your heart wants to be means putting
it out there where the world can judge it—and doing it in the
smartest and most appealing way possible.

Chapter 69
SHIP IT

This is from Seth Godin's blog. I saved it because it rings so true. The title of this post is "On Schedule."

We get a huge benefit from making a simple commitment:

Don't miss deadlines.

The benefit is that once we agree to the deadline, we don't have to worry about it anymore. We don't have to negotiate, come up with excuses or even stress about it.

It won't ship when it's perfect.

It will ship because we said it would.

Once this is clear, the quality of what we ship goes way up. Instead of spending time and energy looking for reasons, excuses or deniability, we simply do the work.

And over time, we get better at figuring out which deadlines to promise. Because if we promise, we ship.

Chapter 70
KILLER INSTINCT, PART ONE

Last year I did a video series on Instagram called *The Warrior Archetype*. One of the points I was trying to make was that physical virtues that we often associate with combat warriors can also be called upon as we fight the interior "war of art."

One of these virtues is Killer Instinct.

I know, I know. Immediate pushback says, "Kill kill = bad bad."

Is it?

I tried to write my first book when I was twenty-three. I spent two years and got 99.9 percent of the way through. I choked. I couldn't finish. I wound up blowing up my marriage and what remained of my sane life, rather than cover those last few strides to the finish line.

Why? No killer instinct.

I couldn't slay the dragon that was that book. Instead, it nearly killed me.

Chapter 71
KILLER INSTINCT, PART TWO

One of the laws of Resistance is that

Resistance is always strongest at the finish.

The example I cited in *The War of Art* was of Odysseus at the end of his voyage home from the Trojan War.

Ithaca was in sight. The ship was so close to shore that Odysseus's men could see the cookfires burning on the hillsides. Their skipper, alas, had chosen this moment to lie down for a snooze. The men knew he had a hide-covered sack that he would let no one touch. They decided to plunder it.

What Odysseus's men didn't know was that the sack contained the Adverse Winds, gifted to their commander by King Aeolus. When the men opened the bag, the winds rushed out in one furious blow, driving the ship back across every league she had traversed on her long voyage home.

It took me years to learn to finish a project. In other words, to develop killer instinct.

Seth Godin prefers the verb "ship." He means if we've been designing the new iPhone for the past eight years and it's finally ready… Ship it!

That's killer instinct.

What, exactly, are we "killing"?

We're killing Resistance.

We're sinking our dagger into the insidious, pernicious, rotten, sneaky, evil force of our own self-sabotage. Our own hesitation. Our own fear of success (or failure).

Killer instinct is not negative when we use it to finish off a book, a screenplay, or any creative project that is fighting us and resisting us to the bitter end.

Steel yourself and put that sucker out of its misery.

Ship it.

Kill kill = good good.

Book Eight

PUT YOUR ASS…
ON THE SPIRITUAL PLANE

Chapter 72

A MODEL OF THE UNIVERSE

In Alcoholics Anonymous, they call it a "Higher Power." I've never been completely comfortable with that term. But I certainly believe that the Material Dimension, upon which you and I dwell, is not the only level of reality that exists.

Where do ideas come from? If we're honest, you and I, we have to admit that we don't know—except that ideas don't come from *us*. A song by Tom Waits, a novel from Elizabeth Gilbert... both artists will confess immediately that the ideas "came to" them.

Homer invoked the Muse. I myself have felt more than once that I was "taking dictation," that a book was "coming to me" from some unseen plane or dimension.

So let me exchange "Higher Power" for "Higher Dimension"—a sphere of reality that exists "above" the Material Plane but that permeates and interacts with this plane.

Still with me?

Chapter 73

THE ARTIST'S SKILL

Let's declare further that the artist's skill (above and beyond the technical prowess of dancing, playing the piano, or crafting a work of fiction) is simply the ability to access that Higher Dimension.

Where did *War and Peace* come from? Where did *Guernica*? Where did the idea for the Eiffel Tower come from?

For sure, it has been my experience that ideas for books not only "come to me" (often unbidden) but actually *seize* me. They take possession of me with a force that I can't shake. In Linda Ronstadt's famous phrase, "I can't *not* do them."

What is this phenomenon about? What does it signify?

If ideas come to us from another dimension of reality, where is that dimension? What do we call it? What does it mean that the artist (and others as well) can somehow access this dimension? How did they acquire that skill?

Chapter 74

A MODEL OF THE PSYCHE

I was first exposed to this model (see below) by my next-door neighbor, the actor and producer Tom Laughlin ("Billy Jack"). But the graphic itself is a fairly conventional representation of the Jungian/Joseph Campbellian concept of the psyche.

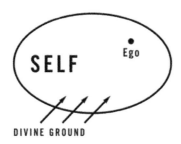

The ego is the small black dot. The Self is the greater circle surrounding it. Adjacent and interpenetrating the circle is the "Divine Ground." What, you may ask, does this have to do with "Put Your Ass Where Your Heart Wants to Be?"

The ego is your ass.

The Self is where your heart wants to be.

The Divine Ground is what powers the Self and renders it transcendent.

Every chapter in this book leads to one final aspiration.

Blow off your ego. Move to your Self.

It may help to realize that the inner transformation called for by every great religion from Buddhism to Hinduism to Christianity to Zoroastrianism is nothing more than this.

Chapter 75

A DEFINITION OF THE EGO

The ego is that part of ourselves that we call "I."

The ego is the part that has a driver's license, that pays taxes, that worries about its kids' futures. The ego is rational. The ego thinks. The ego makes plans. The ego worries. The ego fears. The ego perceives reality through the prism of its own "I"-ness.

When we try to sing or write or dance from the ego, we fall on our face.

It is impossible to sing or write or dance from the ego.

Chapter 76

WHAT THE EGO BELIEVES

The ego believes that the Material Plane, upon which it exists, is the only reality.

The ego believes that time and space are real.

The ego believes it is housed within a physical body.

The ego believes/knows that it will die.

The ego believes/knows that it can be hurt, maimed, mutilated.

Because of these, the ego experiences fear.

The ego believes it is separate from every other ego.

The ego believes it can take an action that harms another person and it—the ego—will be immune from that harm.

The primary emotion of the ego is fear.

Chapter 77

A DEFINITION OF THE SELF

The Self, as Carl Jung or Joseph Campbell might have defined it, is the Greater Sphere of the psyche.

The Self contains the Ego but is many times greater.

The Self does not think of itself as "I."

The Self inhabits a physical body but is not bound to it.

The Self exists on the Material Plane but its true home is Somewhere Else.

The Self contains the Unconscious (Personal as well as Collective).

Dreams come from the Self. Intuition comes from the Self. Ideas come from the Self. Inspiration comes from the Self.

War and Peace came from the Self. The Ninth Symphony came from the Self. The Eiffel Tower came from the Self.

Chapter 78
WHAT THE SELF BELIEVES

The Self believes that death is an illusion. The soul is immortal, and the plane upon which it exists is indestructible. Nothing can harm or destroy the Self.

The Self believes that time and space are not real. The gods travel "swift as thought."

The Self believes that all beings are one and are bound to one another inextricably.

The Self believes that if one being harms another, that being immediately experiences that harm to itself.

Because the Self believes/knows that all beings are interconnected, the Self acts out of care and concern for others.

The primary emotion of the Self is love.

Chapter 79
THE ARTIST'S SKILL, PART TWO

If the artist's skill is the ability to open the pipeline from the ego to the Self—and it is—then "Put your ass where heart wants to be" means exactly that.

Seat your identity not in the ego, but in the Self.

Chapter 80

ADVICE FROM AN ADDICT

This psychic transformation—the relocation of the identity from the ego to the Self— happens when a person with an addiction (to alcohol, to drugs, to self-dramatization, whatever) ceases to be in denial about this and instead declares to him or herself, "I have a problem that will kill me if I don't stop it… and I am powerless to overcome it."

In that moment—the instant when the individual commits to solving the problem, no matter what it takes—her or his seat of identity shifts from the ego to the Self.

In that instant, true change becomes possible. In fact, true change has already begun.

Are you an artist? Then you have made this transition yourself, whether you realize it or not. You have left the ego behind. You are operating from the Self.

In other words, you have put your ass where your heart wants to be.

Are you an aspiring artist? Then this is the transition you are seeking.

Chapter 81

WHAT CHANGES WHEN WE PUT OUR ASS
WHERE OUR HEART WANTS TO BE

We look at ourselves and the world differently once we've relocated the center of our being from the ego to the Self. Yes, we still pay taxes and still participate in politics and still concern ourselves with our children's futures. We have to because we do inhabit the Material Dimension and these concerns are legitimate and honorable and necessary.

But simultaneously we inhabit a different Reality, a reality in which we are at once more aware of our individual gift (and of our obligation to realize it) and of the gifts of an infinitude of others (and our obligation to assist them in realizing their own worth and power).

Here are some of the ways we may act differently, operating out of this new reality.

> An opportunity may be presented to us that we would have jumped at in a prior incarnation—say, to acquire wealth or to achieve great personal or professional recognition—and we may turn it down.

> An enterprise or adventure may capture our imagination—one that entails grave hazard or expense, that may cause distress and anguish to those we love—and we may choose to embrace it anyway.

A revolutionary upheaval may occur in the life of our community or nation and we may say to ourselves, "I must take a stand, even if it means risking everything." Or in the same instance we may conclude, "This convulsion is ego-spawned madness. My proper function is to keep myself and my family safe until it subsides. I will not participate in this state of affairs, nor abet its furtherance in any way."

When we put our ass where our heart wants to be, we may change where we live; we may alter what we do to support ourselves. We may rethink the way we dress or wear our hair. We may shave our skull; we may acquire tattoos—or efface them. We may change political parties, invent new ones, or drop out entirely. Our taste in music, books, art, or movies may change. We may discard longstanding habits and addictions. We may acquire new enthusiasms, make new friends. We may marry or divorce.

We may change the time we get up in the morning and the hour we go to bed at night. We may rethink the people we choose to associate with. We may make over the way we eat or sleep or decide or act. That which we had previously considered important, even vital or indispensable, we may now shed as lightly as a worn-out coat. We may elect to simplify our life. We many choose to live ten times larger. We may change our religion or drop religion entirely.

Those who had admired us, or supported our ambitions in the past, may now turn against us. The violence of their hostility may surprise or even overwhelm us. The people closest to us, our own parents or children, may become estranged from us, or us from them.

Simultaneously we may find ourselves drawn to others whom we had previously overlooked or even despised. We may find ourselves living in another country, speaking another language.

The measures by which we judged a person's or an activity's or aspiration's value or utility may be overthrown. They may become the exact opposite of what they had been. We may come to dread death as we never had before—or lose all fear of it. We may relocate to the center of things or evacuate to the periphery.

Our priorities change when we make the shift from the ego to the Self. Our field of consciousness broadens. We see ourselves no longer as an isolated element in a random or meaningless universe. Instead, our passage through this material dimension acquires significance, even if we can't articulate what that significance is. We sense ourselves as part of a greater cosmos, extending without limit into the past and projecting infinitely into the future.

> We become conscious of our own gift. We no longer doubt this or dismiss it or despise it. Instead, we resolve to serve it. We may still fear personal extinction. We may still worry about our children's futures and the health of our community and nation and planet. But we come at these concerns from a different place and with a different sense of what kind of difference we can make and how and why, or even if we wish to attempt to make a difference at all.

We have become artists, not in the precious sense of differentiating ourselves from others in some imagined superior way, but in the sense of being servants of an intention that comes from somewhere else, even though we cannot grasp what that intention is or what its source may be. We trust this intention some-how, even though we can't say why.

It is no small thing to put your ass where your heart wants to be.

Can you do it? Do you want to? Are you willing to pay the price?

SPECIAL THANKS

To James Rhodes for permission to quote from his April 2013 article for the *Guardian UK*, *"Find what you love and let it kill you."* All rights reserved.

To David Leddick for permission to quote from his book *I'm Not for Everyone* and to Ryan Holiday for letting me cite a passage from his book, *Perennial Seller.* Lastly to Seth Godin, for every blog post he's ever written, specifically "On Schedule."

SARSAPARILLA MEDIA
(sass·per·illa)

My dad's favorite drink was sarsaparilla. He'd come home from work, look at my brother and me and say, *"How about a glass of sass?"* Naming this new company **Sarsaparilla Media** is a way of paying homage to my dad.

Printed in Great Britain
by Amazon